LEEK and PASTA

A HUMOROUS INTERNATIONAL RUGBY ADVENTURE

By Dai Openside

An Oval Publication Limited

ISBN: 978-1-326-06878-3

PublishNation, London
www.publishnation.co.uk

The author has lived in South Wales all his life, but has been fortunate to have travelled the world extensively. He has had a considerable amount of ups and downs throughout. He has had the misfortune of being involved in a serious motoring accident as a teenager. This may have been the cause of his extravagant attitude to life and his extravert behaviour as described in the following adventure.

Passage in Time

A BRIGHT IDEA.

It was mid-February; at about 5:20 in the afternoon as I walked in to the 'Llanover Arms', I turned right and walked into the bar with its '60's decor and other attributes of the building's   two hundred plus year history. It was quite full of the 'on the way home' team. Like most of Wales it's a friendly place with a wide range of people of different occupations, the labourer, teacher, company owner, airline pilot, plasterer, bank executive, retired miner and others of the community, to say all of one! The bar is about eight by eighteen feet. The pub has been owned by the same family for over a hundred years! This is just part of its two hundred year history.

The present landlord John who is as 'laid back' as "Uruguay" but if problems should occur he is assertive as a 'French Centre'. Many years ago John followed his uncle Gwyn as 'captain of the house'. Before stepping up, Gwyn had quite a sporting career while travelling to central Canada to make his fortune in the 1930s. Being an excellent rugby player he was capped by Canada and travelled to Hawaii and Japan, winning in Hawaii but losing twice in Japan but being presented to the Emperor .The good all-rounder also played cricket, playing a touring Australian national Touring team in Canada which included Don Bradman, Gwyn was out for '3'. This I feel is an important 'double' in that he played the most famous cricketer in the world but also met the only head of State that has had two atom bombs drop on his country. I ordered a pint, I then sat down next to an old school friend Geoffrey and his friend, I had never seen before, Huw. Many of the comments flying around the bar were on the major subject of Welsh Rugby, and the following weekends International against the Ice cream Boys' in Rome. I am a supporter of the 'underdog' which on times has been Wales.

We also chatted about many other things as time passed, some more important than others. Then I noticed an advertisement on the back page of the 'Echo' evening newspaper that someone else was reading! Flight and accommodation in Rome £299, Friday and Saturday nights leaving 10:30 Friday morning! I said to Geoff and Huw that seems good, but a little short notice! They both agreed, we all ordered another pint. We continued our conversation and said no more if it. I finished my pint and made my way home about 500 hundred yards away.

The next day I was working at the same place so on the way home I called in the 'Lan'. The bar was quite full; I was greeted by my new acquaintance Huw. I bought a pint and sat next to him. The topic of the following weekends match, Italy in Rome was brought up. We both agreed neither of us had been to Rome, why don't we go this weekend? " OK let's do it! " A new adventure! " Where's last night's Echo"? We called to Hazel who was working behind the bar," where's last night's Echo?" "I think it's been thrown out", she replied, "but I'll check and see if I can find it, when I have a spare moment". Huw and I continued chatting, only having met the night before we had questions to ask about each other, how did we know Geoff? Where did we both live?

After ten minutes or so, "I've found it boys", Hazel called across the bar! I thanked her and reached over the bar for the paper. We both looked at the advertisement with anticipation. We agreed on the expedition, "OK Huw, I'll phone the travel agent tomorrow morning (Wednesday)". "What about the tickets?" Huw said looking me in the eye! "Well its £299 for the trip" I replied, let's say £350 budget, Huw smiled and agreed.

Could I get the time off in such short notice? It was 6:30 on Tuesday evening, the flight was 10:30 on Friday, that's if everything's OK with the travel agent. We chatted about our proposed adventure. If everything went as planned I would arrange every detail, and pay by credit card. Huw would come to see me Thursday morning and pay for his share in cash. This was only the second time I had met Huw, he seemed an upright chap and a customer of the 'Lan' so everything was on.

Wednesday morning I phoned the travel agent, we had the last two places. I did the deal, with two stand tickets it came in at £365 each. Pick up all the information from the representative at the airport. I phoned Huw; "great" he replied and said he would give me the cash at eleven o'clock the following morning.

He arrived at eleven o'clock, gave me the cash, and told me he would arrange a taxi for 8:45 to take us to the airport. That evening I called in the 'Lan' about 8:00. I chatted to one of the guys and told him of the proposed trip, and that I was going with Huw who I had met the previous Monday evening. He smiled, and said with good intentions, he had known Huw for a long time and that he could be a "bit of a handful".

Early that day I had popped in to 'Smiths' [bookshop]. The year before I had bought a very useful 'pocket map' while in Montreal. Could I get one? I was in luck, there was just one left of Rome. These are very useful, about 3 by 4 inches, fold out to 10 by 8 inches, two different size maps of the city and lots of details of places of importance. The information of our stay was limited, where in Rome, what Hotel? How near to the stadium? At this time we were going blind to these details!

As all the arrangements had been made by telephone and to picking up the details and information at the airport, the 3 x 4 inch device could prove vital.

While going to bed that night our local contact with the 'Roman Empire' had crossed my mind, time in question AD0046. A mile from our town, are remains of a Roman marching camp which could accommodate maybe 500 to 900 men and 400 horses! The local, very war like tribe were the 'Silures' hence the size of the touring side. For the coming encounter on Saturday afternoon our local 'Silures' were represented by a Dwayne Peel (scrum half).

-31.30 HOURS IGNITION

I was up at 7:00, looking forward to breakfast, the 'Astronauts' breakfast, steak and eggs! Just the thing for a flight into the "unknown"! As a butcher's son I like " pin bone steak", it may not look good, but is the most tender, costs about the same as fillet, just the job with three fried eggs.

Ready at 8:30, a knock on the door! Huw, with a smile on his face are you ready. I quickly checked my kit, and then turned the gas off! I put the bag in the boot of the taxi and we jumped into the back. The journey to the airport would take forty minutes.

As we trundled along the 'A470', "where are we staying?" "I don't know" I replied. We look at each other with in trepidation! "Look" Huw, I said, "we don't know where we are staying, where the stadium is?" I replied "I hope we are not in a hotel which my friends had bedded down in two years ago! That was 20 miles outside Rome!"

We arrived at the airport; the weather was fresh and windy. The place was full of very happy Welshmen looking forward to the encounter in Rome; a number of fans were already 'flying'.

Finding the travel representative, we were handed two air tickets and an envelope with all other information. We checked in and moved to the departure lounge. "I see some boys from the 'Bwl'; I'll be back in a couple of minutes". "OK, Huw". Time past, now I was in line at the departure gate, after 30 minutes, "I'm sorry, it took a bit longer than I thought! The boys bought me a couple of pints of 'arrow type' cider!".

Making our way across the tarmac to our awaiting aircraft, a rather old looking Boeing 737 airliner in blue, white and yellow which looked it had been painted with a 'four inch paint brush'. We made our way up the steps into the rear of the aeroplane; our seats were in the rear near the entrance door. We tossed a coin for the window seat, Huw won!

The air hostess's went through the 'safety procedure', after she had passed through the 'life jacket' section I pointed out to Huw," 'A' you are usually dead before you hit the water or 'B' the aeroplane sinks pretty quickly!".

The aeroplane took off towards the west and Swansea, it banked and pointed to the east, we looked down at the Millennium Stadium as it levelled off. Like a sling shot we were catapulted at 500 miles per hour towards the Mediterranean and Rome.

Huw and I had only been in each other's company for maybe six hours so the two hour flight was taken up with 'interviewing' each other! As we approached Rome we looked down on the multitude of very high rise flats, we both agreed this would not be for us.

Our part of the world, mines long gone, it is basically semi-rural, "They've even blown the flats in Hirwun up", Huw commented with a smile!" (A sixties attempt at social housing)

-26.00 HOURS TOUCHDOWN

We landed at small airport just outside of the city. As we walked across the tarmac to the airport buildings I was impressed to see a line of five/six De Havilland water bombers in their very bright red and yellow colours, but not many forest fires in February!

Walking into the terminal building it did not seem busy except for the hundred and forty passengers from our aircraft. We quickly passed through customs, out of the entrance; we look at each other with a sense of accomplishment, Rome, or near Rome!

Time to open the envelope and see where we were staying, we look on, the hotels name, then to pocket map. Found it, "Huw, it's near the bus/railway station!" We had no transfer so next stage getting there? No taxis in the rank or anywhere to be seen, other passengers getting onto coaches. We split up to see if we could get a ride to Rome, first objective, second hotel.

I met some guys from Swansea, in the same boat as us! What I could gather they were staying 'out of town'. Then I saw Huw, fifty yards or so away waving his arms and shouting at me to run over to meet him. He had found a group of fans from

'Dowlais' Rugby Club; they had a coach and were going to Rome. "What part?" I asked, "We'll work that out when we are there!" Huw said with a smile, I smiled and said OK.

As we walked to the coach I said to Huw to respect 'Dowlais', this is because although it may be part of Merthyr Tydfil now up until 1975 it was an independent town and in 1815 the centre of iron production of the world.

The coach made its way towards Rome, we chatted to the members of the 'club' about things in general and the forthcoming match and where we were staying. Then a guy on the other side of the aisle called across and said "a couple of the boys are staying there!" We looked at each other and could not believe our luck! Yes luck had been good to us! The coach called at two hotels before our lodgings, as we left the coach we thanked the boys from Dowlais for their hospitality and maybe looked forward to meeting them during the weekend.

The hotel was a large terraced building of four storeys and the front entrance opened straight onto the pavement with large double doors. The front of the building was pained in a light blue which gave it an aspect of ' Mediterranean' style.

We both walked through the entrance doorway along the corridor, decorated to a high degree of taste to a large open space, which was reception. We were greeted by a gentleman in a smart suit," messieurs can

I help?". Huw looked at him with a smile and said "yes", we showed him our reservation documents, he took them, looked and turned and spoke to his female colleague, "memento". A long moment passed the female receptionist picked up a key, walking around the desk saying "messieurs this way". We followed her across the hall up a short staircase to a door; she opened the door with a smile. We looked through the entrance into the room which was quite large, high ceilings and decorated again to a high standard. Enjoying the décor, I looked at Huw, he looked at me and we both said in unison and surprise said 'Double Bed!' As we had not known each other for a very long time, we turned and looked at the receptionist and said to her disappointment "no no!"

The receptionist closed the door we marched down the stairs and across the hall to the desk . The two hotel staff chatted, then the male said "we only have this room left", "no, no" was our answer again!! He then looked at us both, put his arms with flat hands up toward us, "sorry sorry" in explanation! More management discussions took place; he then picked up another key. Following him across the hall and up another short staircase, then down a corridor to another door, this looked the same as the previous room. He opened the door the room was the same as before but with single beds, we all looked at each other and smiled! Then he looked again at Huw and myself and touched his nose! Quite a smell of drains, "don't worry it will soon pass", he said to us!

Again Huw and I looked at each other and we reluctantly moved in. Not quite happy with the situation we started to unpack, although there was not much to unpack, it took about four minutes. "To the bar"! Locking the door, we found the dining room, but no bar! Going back to the reception desk smiling expectantly at the female receptionist I said "bar" "no bar" she replied curtly. We quickly had to 'reassess' the situation. We walked out of the hotel and turned left. After a couple of minutes we came to an intersection in the road, we look left in the distance we could see that the road ended with an open aspect and bright blue sky! I consulted the 'pocket map' which confirmed we were walking towards the central bus and railway stations.

A few yards before this street ended, and the forthcoming stations we found a bar. The establishment was full of Welshmen trying to get a drink! We joined the 'scrum' the bar staff were overwhelmed, trying to pour or make a bottle of beer accessible to the 'mass', it was a 'maul' but without a 'referee'. After a couple of minutes or so the guy in front of us, I think he was from Newport, the appointed 'scrum half' passed two opened bottles to Huw, we had 'position', how or if any money changed hands I cannot recall!

We moved from the pressure to outside pavement, and met a couple of the boys from Dowlais, and planned our next move.

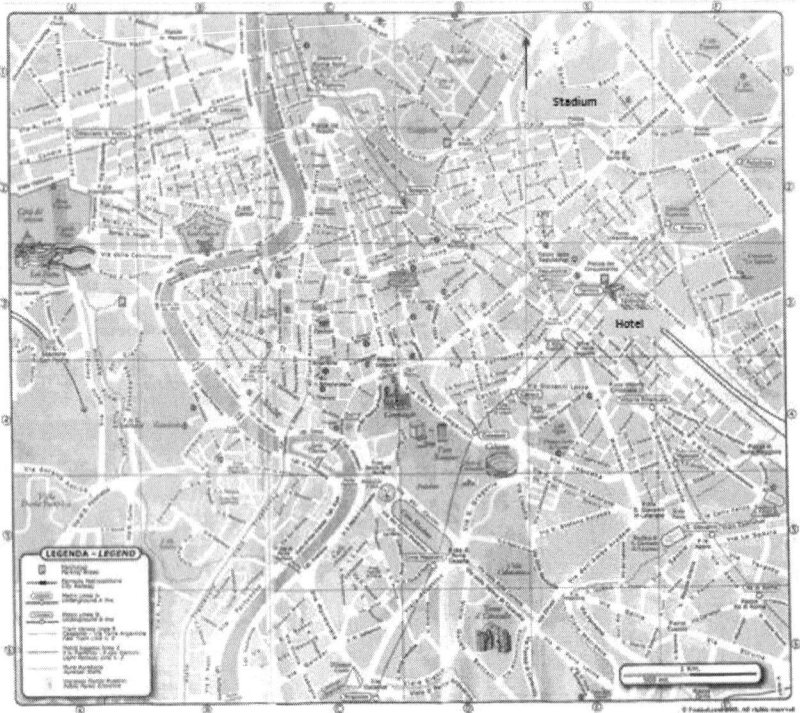

Map of Rome

-24.45 HOURS RECCE

The weather was fine and sunny, much different from the weather at home. We finished our drinks and agreed this was a place of 'continental elegance' with a good atmosphere 'Mediterranean style'. We agreed we should investigate the locality though the adjacent to the bus station with onward looking railway station.

We crossed the road and walked in front of the railway station. We looked at a line of continental express trains facing the open fence. The electric engines, the front part of the trains all in 'bright colours' with their front driving position of all a similar level, their noses sloping down at different anglers aerodynamically towards their front bumpers. This gave me the impression of multi coloured cats ready to pounce.

Locomotives of multi colours red, white, blue, yellow, purples and greens. The exception to this was an engine which was a little longer, out of line, with like a nose-cone painted black, was in white colour and with red crosses on the driver's doors, this was a 'St Bernard' of "Swiss Rail".

Out of the stations area we strolled down the road, which was   wide with buildings of very imposing architecture. After ten minutes our quest for finding a bar, we continued for another five minutes brought no more success, so we decided to make it back to the bus station and to the "Coliseum".

We arrived at the bus station, it was Friday afternoon at 3:30, and the weekend rush hour was starting. Agreeing the situation was a little urgent we would travel by taxi. We quickly hailed a taxi, gave the instructions "Coliseum", "Coloso" was the answer from the smiling driver. The traffic was very busy and to us a little "hairy" from where we were sitting! Overtaking, undertaking, and much beeping of horns. Dangerous to our eyes but all the drivers wanted to go forward in turn, no one collided with anybody else!

We arrived at the 'Coloso' at four o'clock, quickly alighting the cab and running to an entrance, finding that it had just closed. "Bugger!" we both said in disappointment. Maybe going around the other side to another entrance and we rushed around to find it was too closed". We were surprised how near it was to the main busy roads, 3 lanes in some places! We looked and admired the structure of the edifice; the outside was of arches upon round arches, level after level. Huw being an engineer pointed out the structure what seemed to be "concrete" with dressed stone! Well the Romans did invent "concrete".

As we circumnavigated the 'Coloso', we notice a cafe` bar across the road, next to a subway station, actually by the entrance. We crossed the road, made our way to the counter of the busy establishment, it was rush hour on a Friday. Walking to the counter we ordered some ham rolls and a couple of beers, I paid.

We gathered our 'vitals' and walk to the entrance of the café and a possible seat and table. Finding a table for 4 with 2 spare seats we moved towards it. We both looked and smiled at the two young ladies occupying the seats opposite, Huw piped up "senioritis", yes was the reply in a strong 'Cardiff' accent. They both looked up at us. What part of the valleys are you from? Not trying to give our exact identity away Huw said Porth and I said Tonypandy!

The looked up smiled and said, we're from Splott, (actually the "Splottlands" is the proper title for their part of Cardiff). We looked at each other with a little disappointment, to travel across Europe and the first girls we meet actually live 12 miles for our homes.

I swung into action with my only 'chat up line'; I looked them in the eye and said "Do you work in the Tax Office?" (When in the United States it's 'Department of Inland Revenue', or tell the lady in question you are related to "Richard Burton"!). "No" was the answer, "I work in Peacocks" and my friend works in "Howells". Huw came in with "where are you staying?" "In a hotel the other side of the Vatican," one of the girls replied, Huw continued, "What seats have you got for the Match?" "We haven't", was the reply, "We are going to watch the match in the 'Irish Bar'!" Do you know where the

"Irish Bar is? " We both looked with amusement! "Sorry" we replied, "we've only been in Rome a few hours!"

They finished their drinks, smiled got up saying "see you boys" and walked into the entrance of the underground station.

We finished our beer and rolls, by this time the Coloso was lit up and was quite impressive as the evening was coming on. We left our seats walked out of the café and on the roadside opposite to the Coliseum; behind us was quite a steep ridge opposite the edifice. Walking a little way down the road, onto a winding path we were confronted by a steep hill. During our ascent we talked about the girls from 'Splott', "Anyway" Huw said "mine was quite attractive but yours had a face like a "RIPPED DAP" [dap -a running shoe]. I replied," that not a kind thing to say!"

As we neared the top of the ridge the path leads to a narrow road with a row of buildings facing the Coliseum. A bar appeared, we look in at its impressive glass front, and inside it's even more impressive interior 'Deco' and lighting. As we entered this was 'something else' - a real cocktail bar.

Huw ordered 2 beers, "my turn" he said, sitting down we looked through the very large window facing the Coliseum, and the bar was situated at the same height as the top of that historical building. Quite a view of Rome, and a tremendous sunset of carrot red, orange rays with purple streaks of cloud! The waiter brought the beer but in a place like this we should be drinking 'very dry martinis'. We discussed what to do next, back to base, shower, and dinner and find the 'Fountains of Trevi'. Finishing our drinks, we stood up, Huw picking up the bill, "Copulation" he cried with pain in his face! " Eighteen Euro's for 2 beers!"

We left the bar, Huw muttering about he would return the compliment during the forthcoming weekend! We quickly descended the path to the main road, "Look, that bus", it said "Centro Station". We quickly ran to the nearby bus stop as the giant black building on wheels stopped. We jumped on entering through the "out" door. The very large black projectile is quite different from the '132' which comes from Maerdy and goes to Cardiff every 15 minutes.

Payment is made by a card system which you pre-purchase, and then push into machines at a number of points on the bus. During our earlier passing visit to and through the bus station we had discovered this important factor, although we hadn't bought any tickets.

The bus was full, no bus cards, if challenged by an inspector (standard fine 50 Euro's) Huw would show his works ID and give his M D,s direct phone number after 'pleading ignorance'. The captain or driver of this 'land ship', in what it seemed is in a sealed

'Perspex box' at the front left hand side with radio communication and its own oxygen supply.

Five stops on to the Centro bus station, we dismounted as quickly as we could, in five minutes we were in the Hotel. Straight to our room, still the 'drain odour'. We showered in turn, dressed and to the hotel front door in 20 minutes.

Dinner and 'Fountains of Trevi', we hailed a cab I requested our general direction and purpose, "ci" the driver said in agreement! By this time the rush hour gone, 15 minutes and we were deposited in a square with high ornate buildings surrounding it!

Opposite the cab was a restaurant, traditional in style, a marble like finish outside walls and ringed white curtains half way up the window. We looked at the menu in a brass edged case on the wall outside the door, at 66p to the Euro it looked very good value!

As we walked in we were greeted by a waiter immaculately dressed in black trousers and jacket with a white apron. The restaurant had a very clean and neat feel; the walls had white tiles to the halfway point then a deep red finish to the ornately decorated white ceiling. We were shown to a table to the right of the entrance which viewed the length of the restaurant. The table neatly laid, with a white table cloth, complimented by chairs of a fitting style whilst the bar to our right consisted of what could only be called a "Wall of Wine".

After passing compliments with the waiter, Huw declared although we spoke "Ingles" we were actually "Welsh". I requested the menu and two beers, the waiter returned, but had an elderly lady with him, by her manner the person in charge,

She took our order, two medium steaks and a bottle of Chianti. The staff seemed very interested in our interest in rugby which they knew very little, but we explained a little of the "Six Nations Championship".

A waiter brought the wine and carefully opened the bottle, it had a rich, dark red blue colour and it tasted magnificent! Chatting with the staff continued, the steak arrived, we settled down to enjoy a good 'scoff'. The outward part of the steak was a dark red blue in colour, I cut into this outer "case" it was very tender, it revealed flesh of pink and red. I carried out the intersection with an ordinary knife; if you need a steak knife the meat is not very good.

After finishing our 'feast', with some coffee, we split the bill, thanking our hosts for their hospitality and giving us the general direction of the 'fountains'. This old part of Rome has narrow cobbled streets with buildings of at least four/five storeys. As Huw had taken directions he lead the way, there were few people around, the evening was 'getting on'.

Up streets, down streets, back down streets, around corners we arrived. But in such a small square, the fountain was brilliantly lit in a pale orange colour, but surrounded in such high buildings! It reminded me of finding the locks of the 'Glamorgan Canal' behind the "Bunch of Grapes" but with lights. Still not many people about, with me, Huw and some guy, I think walking home it as by now 9:30. We made a wish, threw some coins into the fountain and walked into bar on the left.

The bar was empty and closing, staff consisted of two girls, and we ordered 2 beers. Huw swung into action with the interrogation quickly resulting in that both girls were from Australia on the 'magical mystery tour' of Europe! They were doing it backwards and hadn't discovered Wales yet. One of the girls admitted to having relations in Barry. Finishing our beer, wishing our new Australian friends the best and safe travel, Huw gave one of the girls his phone number and blew a kiss!

The day had been busy! But we had not drunk much beer! Not having a bar in the hotel may have been an advantage, also not to be stuck in "one place"!

We decided to find a taxi, return to base, and find a bar for an hour or so. Finding a taxi was a bit of a problem, we arrived outside the hotel at 11:00.

-16.30 HOURS NIGHTCAP

We strolled down the street from the hotel but in the opposite direction of the Stations. After maybe 200 yards we found a small bar on the opposite side of the road. We climbed up two steps to enter through a single door, the barman greeted us with a smile, and Huw ordered some beers. On the other side of the bar was four guys sitting at a table, they were speaking English! We collect our beer and sat near the 'quartet'.

After a minute or so we introduced ourselves by asking the question, "What part of Wales are you from? " We are not!" Was the reply in a number of very "English accents". "Are you here for the rugby? "Yes", "well what connections do you have with Wales?" "None" was the reply in unison. "We are from Kent". " Why are you in Rome?" "For a good interesting time", "last year we went to Dublin to watch Ireland v France!" Why? " Well English rugby tours can be dull and boring!"

Although they seemed outward going at first, they lacked a little "hwyl" as we say in Wales. They were very interested in us though, asking polite questions about Huw, myself and Wales. They were very hospitable, for being English and they kept both of us in beer for the next couple of hours. It had gone 1:30, we called it quits, we both wished our new friends well and parted company.

A few steps away to our hotel, we made it to our room, still with 'drain odour' into bed and the match tomorrow!

-05.10 HOURS MATCH DAY

"Huw, Huw!" I shouted "its 20 past 9!" I made it to the shower as Huw jumped out of bed. It was a 'dash and splash' followed by Huw. Breakfast finished at 10, we arrived in the ornate breakfast room at about 9:40. It was a full, full continental spread, cheese, rolls, fresh fruit cake, with different coffees, juice and tea. It was a good start to the day.

We chatted and made our plan of attack! Kick off at 2:30, we finished eating at about 10:30. We sat down in the foyer, consulted the 'Pocket Map', the Stadio Flaminio was about, maybe 2 to 2.1/2miles north west of the hotel (bus station). Stepping outside to gauge the weather, it was winter, what clothes to wear? 'Polo shirts' the weather was warm and sunny not rugby weather in Wales!

By now it was coming up to 11:00 so we strolled up to the 'Stations' maybe have a coffee and look at transporting ourselves, via some lunch to the ground. On arrival the bus station it was devoid of buses. It was the central point of a demonstration; in fact no service buses at all! This did not concern us because we had worked out that if we got a taxi to the top of the 'Spanish Steps' this would bring us to a point at the edge of the park, which was the opposite side to the Stadium

The station area was quickly filling with thousands of Italians from all over Rome who had come to protest about the "invasion of Iraq". We had a coffee in the bar we had been in the day before! We left there about 12:00.

The street was devoid of taxis. After ten minutes we manage to hail a lone taxi. We bundled in, Huw giving the orders "foot of Spanish Steps!" We set off, after a hundred yards or so, I asked the 'cabby' how much? He replied 20 euro's, "what" we said in surprise! "You (comments of female genitalia)". This was for a journey of about the same as we had made the night before for 8 euro's. I ordered "stop stop" the cab pulled up, we quickly exited without paying, and then we stood on the pavement and to reassess the situation! The weather was great for a 'cricket match' warm and sunny kick off 2:30, we calculated if we walked across Rome we would have ample time, a pint on arrival, 20 minutes for a sandwich on the way as well!

We set off past the stations in, what we hoped the general direction. The streets became narrow, cobbled roads with tall buildings of many storeys. At varying distances the undulating streets converged in squares, with traffic police with white gloves directing the busy flow, to me something out of the 'Italian Job'! Once or twice we consulted our 'map', and on one occasion enlisted the help of the friendly "carabinieri" officer for directions. Huw and I were quite taken, and I was in the way she fitted her uniform!

Crossing a square there was a sign "Scallnata d Trinita a Monti" – Spanish Steps, this pointed to a narrow lane which was quite steep. We concluded that this lane lead to the top of the steps and therefore to the edge of the Park and our half way objective.

Strolling up the hill we were impressed with when looking into the windows of some very exclusive shops and boutiques with prices to match. We found a small café about two thirds of the way up the hill, as it was about quarter to one, time for coffee! Plus maybe a bite'to eat. As we walked through the café door as the sun shone brightly down the road to meet us. The café was traditional with quite a formal aspect, the front windows with white curtains half way up the windows. The inside with bright white tiles, and again up to halfway on the walls. The counter and till to the side of the entrance door, tables and chairs to 25/30 feet to the end of the room.

Sitting down, Huw put his arm up, a waiter arrived promptly, and dressed smartly in a white shirt, black trousers, and white apron, and looking at the menu I said two coffees and two cakes. We discussed our progress, "well Huw we take about 30 minutes to cross the park, he agreed", it will give us 30 minutes before kick off – and time for a beer!

Finishing our coffees and cake we made our way and to settle our bill. Huw lead and I had the account. I presented the bill to an old lady, the owner, "Metridam". She said in broken English, fifteen euros, I said "No!"

At this time Huw disappeared, using his initiative, and his motto "One for all, all for one, and everybody for himself!"

I answered the lady with the menu and said 8 euros! For some reason the bill had disappeared! "No No" I replied again!

Putting her hands and arms in the air she shouted," Police Police."

I again shouted "No! No!"

She again, "Police Police"

Thinking what to do, I concluded, and made my counter attack! I put my arms in the air and shouted, "Police Police."

The lady put her arms down in surprise and looked at me. I put eight euros on the counter and made a swiftly exited! Reaching the street I look up the hill, I saw Huw about 20 yards away peering out of a shop doorway smiling. I walked up towards him and said you "person without a father!" We continued up the hill, as we climbed the sunlight became brighter. In a couple of minutes we were in open parade at the top of the 'Spanish Steps'.

In the bright sunlight the view was spectacular, looking down on the entire 'Vatican City', the River Tiber and the surrounding parts of the City.

-01.15 HOURS WHAT DIRECTION

Then to a parade, which then lead to a slope, then at the right hand side there was a grass embankment, and quite a high cast iron fence which was the side of the Park, an ornamental gate some hundred yards away indicted the entrance. Suddenly, a growl, a high pitched "whir" as a blue flash passed us at about 3 foot high at quite a velocity. What was that? Huw shouted as the noise died away! A "Ferrari XXYZ" I replied, "We are in Italy!" Huw not a car person, I explained the subject and pointed out the difference from a 'Morris Oxford'.

We strolled down the road and entered the park gates and up some steps onto a path heading north east. The park had a very open plan, very large with undulating wide meadows but with few trees, and stadium not in view! It had just gone one twenty, the sun was shining like a summer's day, and we thought if we could arrive at our destination in thirty minutes it would give us sample time for a beer.

We marched on, after fifteen minutes, still with no view of our goal "we should ask someone for directions!" but a problem, the place was deserted! We found two ladies walking in the opposite direction, Huw politely enquired, but they could not speak English!

We pressed on, as we went over a small hill we found two 'Carabinieri ', I asked this time, they could not speak English either! So we showed them our match tickets. We all smiled and they pointed us down some steps, and over a bridge and some ways further. Huw and I thanked them and we again marched on, time was getting on!

We carried on but a little time later turning a corner, look down at some open gates which lead to a large square. "It was full of very happy, merry welsh supporters".

The square was full of bars, one of which looked very grand, and a lot of empty buses. The supporters were making their way to a road on the right hand side.

We quickly walked down into the square and joined the flow. We found Dai the 'post' and Mike the 'builder', both clients of the 'Lan'. They told us that the stadium was about a mile further up the road. Dai runs the Post Office opposite the pub, Mike lives maybe half a mile from the "Lan", he builds large numbers of houses.

We marched on at quite a pace, Dai told us that the 'Romans' had put free buses on for the supporters due to demonstrations, we said we knew nothing of this. Huw and I agreed that our walk through Rome as far more interesting than a free bus ride, but we had nothing to drink (alcohol), it was obvious our two friends had!

We, with hundreds of eager Welsh supporters were making progress; one supporter was dressed as "Elvis"!   Myself and Huw could not work out why? "Kick off" was getting close, could we get a drink?

Suddenly we came out of the shadowy street and there was the Stadium, built for the 1960's Olympics' hockey and football, it was small but elegant. I asked Dai and Mike where were they sitting, a different place from us. We said "see you later" and parted company. We got our bearings! Huw ran off, he had seen a guy selling bottles of larger from an ice box. He presented me with one, I congratulated him on his initiative he said he had to part with four euro's a bottle.

Through the turnstiles, into a passage and up steps and to our seats. The stand was open, opposite to a large covered stand with the changing rooms. The stadium was constructed of light sandstone which gave an impression of permanence and style! The view was excellent, the sun was shining, behind us, and overlooking this part of the stadium were residences of three storeys, individually spaced out, with views of Rome "I was very impressed".

Eighteen minutes past two the teams ran proudly onto the green turf of the stadium, a surprise to the Welsh contingent in bright Mediterranean sunshine.

This illuminated the red shirts of Wales and the light blue of Italy.

The anthems over, the teams lined up and faced each other. Wales maybe looking at their opponents with utter confidence, as the Welsh supporters could confirm. Who are these 'upstarts', who do they think they are thinking they could they beat the might Wales.

Italy, the new kids on the block! Now part of the 5 nations, now 6 nations, but saying that they had already won since they had joined 2 seasons before! They faced Wales with utter respect, with thought of the 'mighty task' in hand. Without the heritage maybe the 'rugby nation' facing them they were determined to go "full throttle" for the eighty or more minutes facing them!

'Tuned Up' is a fitting description of the so called 'underdogs' of the days encounter, their light blue shirts had a white 'Jaguar' on its front, the Coventry sports car company were their sponsors. They were felling like 'E' Types, like the sports car of the 60s and 70s. Powered by V12's, 48 values, lubricated, not by the best synthetic oil at £100 per gallon but by the best olive oil at £100 a litre and all powered by the best vintage 'Chianti'.

Wales using the 'vichanalicar' description were like 'Rover SD1's', a very good looking and powerful salon car. Outwardly influenced by 'Pinnafarina of Milan' looking like a 4 seater " Daytona " Ferrari and last of the front engine, sports car classics. These Rovers were put together at Rover Way in Cardiff; the motor was a V8 which originally was designed by a motor works in Bavaria. Today lubrication was a combination of 'Larva Bread' from Penclawdd and 'Welsh salted butter', power was from a 'Cardiff beer'.

00.00 HOURS ZERO HOUR

Huw and I looked on with excitement, Wales kicked off, the ball travelling down the pitch, it was gathered by Diego Dominguez Wales waited, and seeing the opportunity the Italian ran forward gaining important yards and time before making his return kick. This stated the Italian team's intentions, no reverse gear!

Within three minutes, prop Giampiero de Carli was the first Italian hero, rolling over the line to score his countries first try of the day! Huw and I were taken back by the pace of this action! Dominguez promptly converted the try!

Wales were startled at their opposition's pressure, and the response was soon. Steve Williams made his second try for his country in twenty five games for Wales; this then was converted by Iestyn Harris.

Pace gathered, Italy charging forward were penalised for two 'inept' challenges into Welsh territory. An opportunity opened and Tom Shanklin the Saracens centre raced clear from sixty yards out to gain his third try for his country.

The Italians counter attacked, after a move by the skipper, Carlo Festuccia in which he drove over from a short distance to level the scores. Again converted by the Argentinean by birth, Dominguez.

In the remaining period before half time both sides conceded penalties. Iestyn Harris and Dominguez being equally successful. In the last moments of the half with the continuing confidence of Dominguez and his team, he 'levelled up' and scored a 'drop goal' which levelled the points. Both myself and Huw, together with our surrounding Welsh fans were very surprised by the so called 'underdogs'. In the Italian changing room as Kerwin the coach gave his recommendations, advice and directions, then the great Enzo Farreri [late motoracing /team owner] appeared!

The team looked on with in trepidation, "Bravo Boys" but a 'Jaguar' on your chest In 1961 the 'E' Type' to me was the 'sexiest' car in the world, so maybe it's OK! The 'Black Stallion of Francesco Baracca' (First World War air ace) on your chest maybe?" "Arrivederci", and the great man was gone!

The second half carried on with the Italians in command. They grounded their third try, Troncon had stolen the ball from a Welshman, and then to flanker Andre de Rossi passed to Matthew Phillips a New Zealander by birth and scored another try for the home side and converted by Dominguez.

We and the surrounding Welsh supporters feared all could be lost, some Welsh supporters who were enlightened by the quality of Italian play were shouting "Italia Italia"!

As a little time passed, the confident Dominguez executed another drop goal. As full time quickly approached our local 'Silure' Dwain Peel with Italy down to fourteen men, touched down a try for Wales. "The whistle blew". Wales had lost by eight points.

+02.10 HOURS SURPRISE

The mood of the Welsh supporters was of utter shock! The Italians were hysterical with the joy of victory. They had treated us with respect and dignity; the better team had won with style and commitment.

We made our way down the open elegant concrete stand. Huw was finding it hard to accept that the upstarts had beaten the 'mighty' Welsh. I was happy that the underdogs had won, by a better organised and free playing team.

As we made our way out of the stadium we soon met Dai the 'Post' and Mike the 'Builder' who were both in a traumatic condition. Their comments were "only if" or "very lucky" as we made our way down the road, we two hours or so before had very confidently made our way to the 'Stadio Flaminio'. We were surrounded by our compatriots which seemed to be all contemplating suicide, the "Elvis" impressionist with his black wig was out of control running around in circles and very drunk.

We made our way at quite a pace and then met some guys from Merthyr (Dowlais). "How are you getting back to base?" Huw enquired, "the same way we got here!" was the reply! Although the bus strike was on (expect for the free buses) but underground was still operating.

After ten minutes or so we arrived at the underground station. With hundreds and possibly thousands of fans of both nationalities we made it to the platform to an awaiting subway train. We just managed to push ourselves inside; it was like "Tokyo" but without any railway staff to push you in, but with even more passengers. Huw was two foot in front of me, maybe two passengers managed to push in behind me. It was quite intimidating not possible to move your body just your head. I turned my head just to see the carriage door close, Huw is a little shorter than me, I turned my head back to the original position but he had disappeared into the mass and was nowhere to be seen!

The train moved its way to Centro Station. It felt as if we were all the lubrication in a condom as the carriage made its way forward, we were tadpoles waiting to escape! I looked at a map on top side of the carriage; it told me we were five stops away from 'Central'. We stopped at the first two stations, some people managed to get out, but no one got on. The next two stations the doors did not open at all!

The heat and pressure in the condom was immense! We arrived at Centro the doors opened and 'ejaculation' we gushed like tadpoles up the steps into the warm Italian sun light.

Where's Huw? I first went to the entrances to the underground, no sign of him! I walked across the road to the bar we had been in a couple of times before, the place of the 'scrums'. Not so crowded today, but the atmosphere was dull, many fans some of who were nearly crying! many many comments of "if" and "only"!

I sat down and had a beer, I made comments of "the best team had won" one or two fans agreed, and many more didn't! I had another beer thinking Huw possibly would turn up! He didn't!

I strolled the five hundred yards to the Hotel, made my way to the room, still no Huw! The room still had a 'drain odour'. I decided to have a 'kip' and again wait for Huw.

+03.55 HOURS SINGLE OPERATION

At eight still no sign of Huw, so I had a shower, put a clean shirt on and made it out for some dinner. Turning left after leaving the front door of the Hotel it put me in the general direction of the stations but at the cross roads I turned right instead of left. I strolled down the quite wide street to an intersection, this road was very busy.

Turning left I found car dealerships and a number of family run bars and restaurants. I look at the menus on the walls outside; the prices were considerably less than the night before. I decided on one, a door between two shop windows, from outside deco as usual, rail and curtains half up the windows. I peeped over the window rail, the place was crowded with what I took for locals eating and chatting with great 'gusto'.

I made my way in. I was greeted by an elderly waitress "bonjorno", a table for one please are inglese?" was the reply, are no "Welsh" was my reply. Her manner indicated she was the person in charge, she lead me through the very crowded room and found a place, table at rear of this small restaurant.

Ordering a beer I was given the menu. Minutes later madam returned, I ordered chilli pasta, pork chops and asked her advice about a bottle of white wine! I was enjoying the 'vibrant atmosphere' in front of me a group of four guys who seemed to be on a 'boy's night out', with a table full of wine and Italian food.

On the far side, to the right of me were a couple, maybe on a romantic night out, both very well dressed. He in a smart very well cut suit, she in a super dress, shoes to match, jewellery that was impressive, a body and looks the boys would climb 'Everest' for!

I enjoyed the event with all the Italian 'vigour and charm'. Finishing with a cup of coffee I paid the bill, thanked madam and made it back to the Hotel. It had just gone eleven as I opened the bedroom door, a little drain odour, but no Huw. I made if for bed.

+16.45 HOURS REUNITED

I opened my eyes as sun shone through the gap in the curtains, and I turned my head and there was Huw sleeping in the bed next to me. I slowly got up, had a shower and woke Huw. Before he had a shower he reported his exploits the night before. After leaving the 'Centro' he had ended up in the 'Irish Bar', well I think I hadn't missed much!

We made our way to breakfast chatting at what the possibilities for some action before the plane home. I had quite an open mind, Huw suggested the Vatican, myself not being religious I as a little indifferent but unable to put an alternative suggestion together.

At ten fifteen we finished breakfast and I picked my camera up from our room. We left the Hotel, quickly hailing a taxi. It was a bright sunny Sunday morning, the traffic very quiet, we arrived at just the other side of the river Tiber to the 'Vaticano'. Huw paid the cabbie with the last of his euros, or so he said!

+18.55Hours THE BLESSING

We crossed the river and up the incline of the Playa San Pedro. The Vatican City is quite large but our main interest was the 'Sistine Chapel' so we joined a queue, due to being early in the day in was quite short. We entered the chapel; to me I was surprised of its epic size and height! The decorations and paintings by Michael Angelo impressed me in its colour and detail. Huw was impressed, as an engineer how the place was built in the first place! After walking around for 30/40 minutes that was enough and we should look for a beer and a sandwich. As we made our way out of the side entrance to the chapel there was a huge crowd in the square looking towards the large building on the left. We both thought what is this about? Then the crowd cheered, we looked up to what seemed to be a small window and a man in a white cassock waving his arms. He spoke into a microphone, either in Latin or Italian! What we could make out," the invasion of Iraq" or" the victory of the day before over the Welsh". He blessed the crowd, me and Huw and we made our way. We walk down the slope to the River Tiber, crossing at the Pont Vitte En (as in Pont-y-pridd).

+19.15 HOURS SANDWICH

Beer and a sandwich, reaching the other side of the bridge we look across the road to the right hand side. Yes another typical, as described earlier a family looking bar/café. Huw opened the door and in we went the entrance door to the left of a large window. Looking onto this was a number of chairs and tables for four to six persons. Behind there was a wide counter, below the counter was a glass refrigerated case filled with all types of savouries, ham, cheese, cakes and bread. To the side of the counter was a corridor with a line of tables for two along its wall. Huw and I sat at a table to the right hand side of the counter, with a good view of the main part of the café.

First we ordered two beers before making a choice of what to eat. Behind the counter, three guys in white coats, one elderly and two much younger, these turned out to be the owner and his two sons.

While our beers were being poured we introduced ourselves to the staff. They enquired what had brought us to Rome. "The Rugby" we replied, "are you lost!" was the reply, they continued saying they didn't know much about this subject! I nominated Huw to inform them of the delights of the 'oval ball'.

On our arrival at the café there was only two other customers, but now the place was filling up with Welsh rugby fans. It seemed we were able to help the 'atmosphere' in conversations with staff and customers alike. We brought the conversation around with the staff of immigration to Wales by Italians, in the café trade from the beginning of the twentieth century up until the beginning of the Second World War. Families being divided at this time of war, the naturalised members of the family were conscripted into the armed forces the others interned in the Isle of Man. We pointed out our town once had twenty Italian Cafes but now only four.

In between our table and the counter ran an entrance to a corridor, tables on our side which ran to the toilets. I made a journey to the toilet, a couple of tables down the corridor I passed a young attractive dark haired young lady who was busily writing in a note book. On my return, as I passed her I said 'hello', she smiled and returned the compliment, "English", "No" I replied "Welsh" and smiled, surprisingly she said, are "the rugby, you lost!". Looking at an opportunity for some interesting input I asked her if she would like to join us. "Maybe later, after I have finished writing", answering in perfect English, I smiled and said OK.

Returning to my chair I reported my find to Huw, "ah" he said, "I have been watching her since our arrival", his chair was pointing up the corridor behind me!

A few guys from Dowlais appeared, we greeted them, they indicated their disappointment at yesterday's result, I told our friends behind the bar to get them all a beer and put it on our 'slate'. This in thanks for their hospitality of days before!

Huw ordered us another beer, number four, NB these are not pints but half pints (approx.). As these were past to us I order a couple more ham and cheese sandwiches. We were having a good time, it was one twenty, plenty of time to be at the Hotel at just before four for the pickup' to the airport.

The young lady, some minutes later moved to a table adjacent to ours, we both greeted her with "Hi" and she returned to compliment with a smile as she sat down. "Would you like anything, something to drink or eat?" She smiled again, I looked over to one of the guys behind the counter, "It's OK, give the lady whatever she would like!" She smiled looked at the guy in return smiling, and ordering a beer and a ham and cheese Panini.

I swung into action with "Do you work in the Tax Office?" with a smile the reply was "no". Her beer and Panini arrived, she was now a little more relaxed, and she told us she worked at the Tourist Board, hence her very good English. I introduced myself and Huw; she said her name was Barbara.

Barbara's position with tourism she said enabled her to be aware of the weekend's rugby event. She introduced us to the owner and his two sons.

The place was 'buzzing', we asked the owners to have one on us! First they declined, but after more persuasion they all had a coffee and a cake!

Chatting to Barbara, more beer, the passing of more Welsh fans, a good time was being had by all! After a second beer Barbara said she had to leave shortly to meet her boyfriend at three thirty. The atmosphere and hospitality in the bar by all was still continuing at a pace.

Barbara looked at her watch, stood up, looked at me and Huw with a smile, she thanked us for our hospitality, and the entertaining time, we both kissed her on the cheek, she waved as she went through the entrance door as she left.

The time was passing, things were carrying on at a reasonable pace so I ordered another beer, the chat and 'banter' continued. Finishing our beers we asked the time? " 3:45" one of the guys called across the counter. "copulation" Huw commented loudly! "It was time to go!" Meeting time at our hotel was just before four, but we were the wrong side of Rome!

I asked for the bill, the cost of four hours drinking, food and our 'hospitality' to the staff and to the citizens of Rome. Actually it was my debt as Huw only had two euro's. The owner looked at me with a warm smile, I accepted it was a tourist area he said seventy six euro's! He looked at me again and said fifty five will be OK, thanking greatfully him I gave him three twenty euro notes.

I indicated we had to be the other side of Rome in fifteen minutes, asked for directions to a bus stop, "round the corner and up the hill fifty metres". As we passed through the door we thanked them all for their generosity and hospitality.

+23.35 HOURS LOST TIME

Around the corner, up the hill we arrived at the bus stop as one of the large black buildings on wheels with 'Centro' on the fronted stopped! We both jumped on, still travelling with no means of paying. Although the bus was full, not quite so crowded but with no seats available. As we had rushed in Huw brushed up against a guy, he said sorry. The guy turned, faced Huw and said, "It's OK" in an American accent. The bus pulled off, the three of us were standing quite close together holding on to the hand rails.

Huw turned to me saying "doesn't he look like Harrison Ford", I thought maybe! Huw looked at him and said "We're from Wales and we've been in Rome for the Rugby," "Yes" the American said, and "you lost!" We both agreed in disappointment, Huw continued, "What are you doing in Rome?" I'm at the Embassy" he replied, in a very kind way, due to the state we were in, and diplomatic way (sorry for pun).

Huw continued, "Well Harrison, I've enjoyed all your films especially 'The Temple of Doom' did you do all the stunts? Our new friend Harrison looked and nodded! My comments was less informed as Huw's, but I looked him in the eye, and enquired "did he know who designed your hat in the films?" he looked at me with question and he smiled, "well the guy is from Aberdare! I commented. Twelve miles from where we live! "Harrison what's the time?" Huw asked, "Its 5 after 4" he replied with a smile. Only 5 minutes late of our deadline!

The bus made its way through some very narrow streets; I was impressed with the speed and the small female driver in the left hand side Perspex box who was piloting this monster! The banter continued, Huw and Harrison were getting on fine, Huw knowing a considerable amount about his life, even when he was a carpenter, that's Harrison not Huw! The bus drew into 'Centro', we had travelled next to the door, we poured out first, we looked at the station clock it was four twenty, we turned our heads back, ' Harrison' had disappeared!

We quickly walked out of the bus station, across the road down the street before we would turn right to the Hotel. Half running down the road, we didn't think we were that late and turned right. Looking down the road we saw two men in the distance they were carrying a small suitcase with clothes trapped in the edges and a rucksack.

We met them, they were two travel couriers, and were not very happy. "You late, the bus to the airport went 30 minutes ago, what happened? They enquired. "We had a great time visiting the Vatican we called into a bar for a sandwich at quarter to twelve and all of a sudden it was quarter to four", I said with a smile! "You'll have to get a taxi" taking the initiative I quickly pipe up, "but we haven't got any money". Look he said with an open hand "I've only got these eighteen euro's", I took it out of his hand and thanked him for the loan, while Huw hailed a taxi! They hurried off; giving the impression that eighteen euro's was good value for alleviating the problem.

The taxi pulled over and stopped; the drive got out, took our bags and placed them in the back of the cab. The car was quite interesting, not too conventional. A Fiat "Multipa", more a type of people carrier, quite upright, two head lights, just under either side of the wind screen, the bonnet straight and flat before dropping down to a radiator grill with two more head lights either side looking like a smile! Clarkson and his team had previously made it a 'Car of the Year'.

Inside more 'Italian Style'. Two rows of three seats, each seat was made of plastic leather like material, black lower part, grey upper with red piping! The gear stick or leaver was situated to the drivers right in the middle front of the dash board, this seemed to be based on the 'espresso coffee machine' as it was surrounded by vents and shapes in a cream plastic. The interior gave an impression of a large space with carpets of dark green. The insides of the doors were in two shades of a lighter green with flecks of purple material to me like a sweater that highlighted and projected Sophia Lorraine's assets in a 1950s film. So we jumped into the back of 'Sophia' and sped off to the airport. "Huw we got away with it!" "Yes" he replied, "the flight is at six thirty, plenty of time, "I confirmed. The effects of the beer were wearing off, Huw and I chatting as we road to the airport.

A thought came across my mind, "Huw have you got the air tickets?", "No, you have" was the reply. "Have you got your passport?" He put his hand in his inside pocket and produced it; I definitely did not have mine!

We looked at each other and shouted "Stop, pull in", the driver looked in his rear mirror with alarm! "We have to check my coat and the bags" I said. The car pulled to a stop, Huw and I both quickly jumped out of "Sophia" opened the rear door and inspected my coat and the bags. Huw checked his rucksack, I checked my coat, but to no avail! I remembered putting the air tickets and my passport in the outside pocket of my coat. We looked at each other and said ''copulation!" realising that they had been stolen!

Not to impeded progress we climbed quickly into 'Sophia'. She was started and we were on our way again and informing the cabby of our dilemma and situation. He responded with a shrug of his shoulders and a confirming smile of respect in the rear view mirror! We continued, Sophia and its occupants trundling through the streets of Rome. I leaned forward, "how far to the airport?" "Twenty minutes" was the reply.

A thought crossed my mind; I again lent forward and asked the cabby "which Airport?" "Ah, Leonardo De Vinci" he replied.

To sum up events of the last twenty minutes:- Late behind schedule; therefore thrown out of Hotel; in taxi and not the bus to Airport; Discovering our air tickets for me and Huw plus my passport – stolen;

And to confirm our situation we were twenty minutes from the 'wrong' airport (not cabbies fault, How's original instructions).

"It's the wrong airport Huw", we consulted our 'pilot' it was "Ciampino" airport we need. By this time, he the (cabby) was getting a little 'wound up', but he seemed a patient man, he turned 'Sophia' around and we sped off to the correct airport.

The route we took was through the suburbs, lots of very attractive white houses with red terracotta roofs. It took twenty minutes or so and we arrived at the correct airport, we clambered out of 'Sophia', our very accommodating cabby took our bags out of the car. We smiled as we paid him, and thanked him for being so understanding.

+24.15 HOURS CARABINIERI

We hurried into the airport and found the travel courier again! After our earlier meeting to our surprise he was understanding and helpful. Explaining the situation, he smiled and gives us both new boarding cards; we again thanked him after giving me directions to the desk with two Carabinieri behind it to sort out the passport problem.

I presented myself to their desk, I said "hello!" They smiled and said "English", not to complicate things I agreed. I explained as best as I could my situation about having my air tickets and passport stolen. In response one of them reached for a form, the other looked at me and said "VATICARNO" I nodded and said "yes". They both were very 'laid back' at the situation.

The form was one side of paper, it was quite short and to the point, I quickly filled it in and gave it to the understanding policemen. I moved to the departure lounge to join Huw who had by this time had got a couple of beers and was talking to Mike the 'Builder' and Dai the 'Post' who were on a different flight. Both guys thought the position myself and Huw had got into was "very funny".

Our flight was called; we quickly finished our beer and made our way to the Gate. We walked across the tarmac up the steps onto the aircraft for our passage home.

By this time we both were quite tired; we had had a busy three days. The flight passed quickly, the seat belt light came on!

+28.15 HOURS SOFT LANDING

Then the message over the tannoy said in a few minutes we will be landing at Cardiff. "Tom Jones", "Shirley Bassey"," Richard Burton", "Roald Dahl", "Tyrone Booth", "Barry John", "Doctor Price", "Tommy Farr", "Captain Morgan", "Jack Daniel", International Airport.

We left the aeroplane walked down the tube into the airport itself. I was concerned with what was going to happen next!   There was no Customs Officers, so I walk through with Huw. We picked our bags up walked out of the airport to find a taxi.

Forty minutes later we were in the "Lan" having a pint. As I found out later Dai the Post and Mike the Builder, at this time were still on the tarmac in Rome awaiting their delayed aeroplane to return home!

Huw and I parted company, happy of our exploits during the interesting and eventful weekend. I had a day off the following day, while Huw was still on the 'sick'!

Author's Note

I would like to thank the gentlemen of the Llanover Arms and people of Rome for their hospitality in contributing to this adventure.

Sadly 'Dai the Post' passed away a short time after.